This is the book you wi
your boss would read.

FAILURE OF LEADERSHIP

THE STATE OF BUSINESS AS USUAL IN AMERICA

By

J.P. ABBOTT

Library of Congress Control Number

ISBN: 979-8-9915896-0-4

To My Readers

———————————————

Feel free to read chapters separately in any order you like.

And fair warning: I am a social critic, so don't expect me to mince words. If you don't like foul language, you will be offended.

That said, if I can in any way improve the lives of people working in America—even one life—I will have succeeded in my mission.

So, read if you want to. Or don't. No one's forcing you to be better than you are.

Prologue

Part of this book was written before the 2020 pandemic. As the virus progressed, killing millions worldwide, to my astonishment masks and vaccines themselves were somehow called into question. And corporate "leaders," upset by the situation and feeling out of control, began insisting that their employees work in dangerous office, retail, and food service environments throughout 2020 and 2021.

Some claimed they were "essential businesses"—a very loose designation in many states. Some companies had multiple outbreaks. Some were transparent about this, others were secretive. If employees died or almost died in the hospital, the silence was deafening.

Many companies took government PPP (Paycheck Protection Program) "loans" designed to keep people employed, but they laid off staff anyway. No one ever checked, and the companies never had to pay those "loans" back. Notably, many who benefited from the PPP decry "socialism" and rail loudly against "government handouts."

Given the varying corporate responses, I took great interest in how "leaders" behaved during the COVID-19 outbreak. And although this book was not originally designed to be political commentary, it must be pointed out that some of the worst leaders in America are those who completely ignore the expertise, research, recommendations, and advice of, not only their most qualified and smartest staff, but world-renowned scientists and the entire medical community.

By their own actions, they have proven that in corporate America, party affiliation can be used as a litmus test for leadership ability—or complete lack thereof.

This book was picked up again and finished in 2024, during an election cycle that again puts a spotlight on leadership, as the arguably most selfless leader in American history has declined his party's nomination in favor of saving democracy from those who have a written plan to end it called Project 2025. This jaw-dropping choice by President Joe Biden, one of the most extraordinary leaders in the world to date, impacted me greatly and was frankly the impetus that made me truly want to finish this book.

So, I did.

Chapters

═══════════════

Chapter I

The Demotivated Workforce

If you would take a minute away from your ridiculously busy American work schedule to observe your surroundings, you would see lots of other people like you forcing themselves to go to their jobs every day, dreading Monday mornings, and speeding home bumper-to-bumper every weeknight.

On your commute, you'd see six or eight lanes of crumbling highway infrastructure teeming with thousands of vehicles.

Trucks full of blue-collar men in dirty caps holding quart-sized cups of coffee in huge rough hands, stiff and beaten down from using their strong bodies every day to provide for their families. Speeding women in cheap SUVs managing every life detail for their husbands, children, aging parents and bosses, sneaking two minutes to apply mascara or lipstick in their visor mirror at stoplights while they drop children off at daycares, schools and extracurricular activities, then racing to make it to their own jobs on time.

Stoic white-collar men and women of every age alone behind their wheels, driving through Starbucks or Dunkin Donuts to get a quick caffeine fix so they can make it through another day of kissing ass all day long. Young people struggling to get their careers off the ground by working at two minimum wage jobs, and doing anything to make ends meet—only to learn they can never pay off exorbitant and crippling student loan debt or afford to buy their own homes.

If you live in a city with mass transit, like Chicago, New York, or Washington DC, you'd see the same sights, except instead of driving, you'd see people frowning and scowling over smartphones on trains, buses and subways.

These are the "lucky" people in America, because "they have jobs."

Or maybe not.

Keep looking as you drive by sterile office parks with bushes trimmed into meatball shapes, shoddy commercial buildings with sprinklers watering grass even while it rains, and rundown strip malls plastered with poorly-designed company logos on faded signs shouting false promises to no one in particular. And parking lot after disintegrating asphalt parking lot lined with rows of anonymous employee cars looking like they'd like nothing better than to put themselves in neutral and roll away.

Inside these individual, silent buildings, companies full of people are living out painful dramas of betrayal, sabotage, and emotional abuse every single day. And it doesn't have to be that way.

Chapter 2

People Who Treat People ...As Expendable

What makes up a company? People do, of course. And these people pretend every day that it's "not personal, it's just business."

Workers spend the majority of their lives in misery trying to make a buck and pay their bills while their "leaders" abuse them and those around them, either behind their backs or right to their faces.

Bad owners and managers gather like a horde of crows (also known as a murder, how appropriate) behind closed doors to criticize whoever happens to be out of favor at the moment, blaming them instead of actively researching what's really going on at their shitty companies, proactively solving company problems, and creating a positive vision for others to follow.

You know, like they **should** be doing.

According to pre-pandemic Gallup research, only around 31% employees claimed to be "actively engaged" and enjoying their jobs. That leaves the majority of people "checked out" or sleepwalking through their days without any energy or passion for their work.

Gallup research says these people might be hurting companies' growth trajectories the most. Gallup says: "To engage their workers, companies need to focus on putting high-performing managers in place and creating development strategies that maximize employees' strengths."

Wait a minute, I can almost hear a company "leader" right now—or perhaps a hand-picked ass-kissing middle manager—groaning as they read this research while taking **no** responsibility for the company atmosphere they've created based on distrust, fear, uncertainty, and misery.

A sad state of affairs indeed, and leaders get an F for this. Go back to class, pull yourselves up by your bootstraps because you are **not** making a passing grade. And everyone knows it except you.

Furthermore, since employee salaries and benefits make up such a huge percentage of your company dollar outlay, don't you think you should focus more on how to make your employees better, instead of throwing a money-bandage on the problem by hiring some new consultant or HR professional to clean house or hire "better" people? Then actively demotivate **that person** through your continued crappy, thoughtless, careless leadership? Blaming yet another "failed employee" on them or someone else instead of **yourself**, which is squarely where the blame belongs?

According to the Society for Human Resource Management, salaries as a percentage of operating costs can range from 18-52%. If you run a for-profit company that doesn't have huge capital equipment or inventory costs, chances are you are spending up to **50% of your budget** on people you're abusing instead of motivating.

Not too smart, are you?

But you think there's always someone new ready to put their butt in one of your chairs for your lousy low salary. You think there are plenty of qualified people out there looking for work, scrambling to work for your crappy company, so you task your HR people to go find them and pay them the least amount of money possible.

You never consider your turnover costs—**especially** the high cost you're paying in terms of customer brand loyalty and referrals.

Yes, your customers really do notice that you've had five people in that position in the last three years. And yes, your online reviews are read by more than just prospective employees.

But it's not **just** your reputation. It's also actual dollars that you are pissing away due to your bad behavior.

Research from Center for American Progress, citing 11 research papers published over a 15-year period, determined that the average cost to a company of turning over a highly skilled job can be more than 200% of the annual compensation for that role once training costs, lost productivity and hiring expenses are counted.

This could mean tens of thousands of dollars per employee.

And even replacing low-skilled people can cost you. Some sources say it can cost around 16% of their annual salary to replace your lowest-paid people each time one quits.

Disengagement—now called "quiet quitting"—is also expensive. Gallup estimated that a disengaged employee costs an organization approximately $3,400 for every $10,000 of salary, or 34% because of days they call in sick and time they waste on the job because they hate you.

Before the pandemic, in some industries, as many as 75% of workers were open to or were actively searching for a new job opportunity. During the pandemic, it got worse. Remember the "great resignation?"

According to an article in The Atlantic, "in May of 2021 more Americans quit their jobs than any other month on record going back to the beginning of the century, according to the Bureau of Labor Statistics. For every 100 workers in hotels, restaurants, bars, and retailers, about five of them quit last month.

But it wasn't just low-wage workers eyeing the door. In May of 2021, more than 700,000 workers in the bureau's mostly white-collar category of 'professional and business services' left their job—the highest monthly number ever."

Post-pandemic, there are still many headlines about how hard it is to find qualified workers.

But here's the thing. The true cost of your employee turnover cannot be generalized because it depends on the unquantifiable value of each lost employee's longevity, salary and irreplaceable "tribal" company knowledge, and how badly your high turnover damages your company's reputation and efficiency.

If you want to retain good people, you should both 1) treat them right and 2) pay them what they are worth. Wages—except for yours—have been flat since the 1970s.

That means pay them, not yourself.

According to the <u>AFL/CIO</u>, "CEO pay continues to outpace the pay of working people. In the past 10 years, CEO pay at S&P 500 companies increased more than $340,000 a year to an average of $14.8 million in 2019. Meanwhile, the average production and non-supervisory worker saw a wage increase of $836 a year, earning on average just $41,442 in 2019." Pathetic.

Don't even get me started on **stock buybacks**. Shame on you!

And regarding your insipid ideas about "employee appreciation"—well, what employees **don't** need is a birthday card passed around for everyone to sign, another pizza Friday, or an awkward mandatory "motivational" company event where everyone competes at some stupid game or other. If you really want your employees to be motivated instead of looking for another, better job, you can start by paying decent wages and bonuses. And then spend another **zero** dollars by **actually appreciating them**.

Employees—**people**—need individual attention to their work, they need to know how they fit into the company at large, they need a sense of accomplishment, and they need the structural barriers to their job productivity removed.

That's also called "leadership" or "management" in case you are completely unfamiliar with it.

NOTE: If you're one of the companies who cut positions and outsourced people overseas, keep reading. You can expect to fail, and are failing already even if you haven't quite discovered how much your customers hate this, and the fact that they will jump ship for the first competitor who will provide **real** service delivered by empowered employees that they can talk to in person **quickly** rather than being routed through a frustrating, enraging circular phone system.

Your customers want personal service from real people. They don't want to push fifteen numbers to reach absolutely no one, or stay on hold "waiting for the next available customer service person" for hours when in reality no one will ever answer. Or in the current vernacular, a "doom loop."

Nor do they want to finally get transferred to a call center employee in a foreign country where they might get cut off or be told that "a manager will have to call you back." Which they never do.

By the way, my apologies to people in other countries, this isn't about you **at all**. It's not about the cultural and language differences, it's about your lack of empowerment and training by "company leaders" to actually solve problems and satisfy customers.

It's about poor leadership.

Chapter 3

Hiring Practices

You'd think if a business was still in business they'd be good at hiring. But not so much.

While they are whining about "no one wants to work," companies are forcing people to fill out their long online applications rife with technical problems, then allowing AI to throw applications out before a human has ever even seen them based on questionable criteria.

For instance, employers' bad HR hiring practices demand that people have the **exact same experience** that will be required in their new position rather than finding people with the right skillset and outlook. (Um, **obvi** this leaves you with an extremely small pool of people to choose from—pretty much just people that used to work for you or possibly your shitty competitor.)

Conversely, other employers think they can hire a person right out of college with zero experience and throw them into any position, no matter what skill level is actually demanded by the job. This usually happens because they are cheapskates that think they can get younger people cheaper. Do you think they will be "just as good" as anyone else? Or do you even care?

Some of these inexperienced people will work out—someday—but their work will probably be subpar for several years through no fault of their own. And after they have gained the experience they needed, they will leave for a better job and you will have to start all over again. Duh.

Know this: Your customers will know your reputation as an employer. And you can lose customers because you promised expertise but actually delivered inexperience and inefficiency.

Have you considered hiring great people with the right amount of experience whose skillsets match the job requirements, then training them in the specifics related to your industry? And after that, actually rewarding them and inspiring them to stay instead of leave your sorry ass? Could have had a V8.

There are so many articles about why people leave companies that I'm just going to make a list of some of them to save you the trouble of Google searching or actually having to crack open a management book:

- Your workplace demands too much with too few people. There's too much pressure, deadlines are too tight and resources are not provided.
- Your employees don't make enough money, and on top of that, they are unappreciated for the efforts they put forth.

- Staff feels they cannot take time off—even for a sick day—and especially not for a needed break or vacation. You are required to check in even on your days off.

- Your company does not support creativity or innovation and does nothing except copy competitors.

- Your company forces everyone to pretend to be happy and say "yes" to everything regardless of what's actually happening.

- Your employees are performing thankless tasks, they can't stand their toxic colleagues and they feel depressed by your inattention and lack of caring.

- Your employees are worried about your financial stability or your lack of ethics and bad business practices.

- You've allowed your middle managers to create a hostile work environment, including unwanted sexual attention, unfunny "jokes" and/or verbal abuse.

- Your company treats everyone equally rather than rewarding individual effort.

- Your company doesn't recognize accomplishments or make things fun. It tolerates poor performance.

- Your company promotes mediocrity and hires and promotes the wrong people.

- Your company makes a lot of stupid rules.

- Your company never shows people the big picture or lets them pursue their passions.

But the most important takeaway is this: **People don't quit companies, they quit bosses.** That means you.

Chapter 4

Toxic "Boss" Work Personas

Ignore this entire chapter if you don't want to engage in any negativity today. It was written for a couple of reasons—1) to vent and 2) to illustrate what is wrong with most companies. Toxic boss personalities are the crux of the problem, and if you see yourself here, I'm not surprised.

A bad company is created by more than just the bad leaders' behavior. Leaders who hire, keep and even reward **other people's** bad behavior are multiplying the company's problem.

Have you met any of these people? Have you worked for them? Worse yet, have you **been** one of them?

Personas or archetypes are what we take on when the atmosphere is toxic. Only great leaders can stop bad behavior at their companies—and only by behavioral example, not edict. Also, they must fire bad apples early, before they spoil the barrel.

These personas are not even close to being inclusive—and some are just downright catty because it was never "just business" my work life was always personal. Every single person I have asked feels the **exact same way**.

These personas are based on my experiences as a consultant working with dozens of client companies, as a small business owner, and as an employee through multiple decades of work since I was 14-years-old at my first job in the 1970s. No doubt everyone can contribute their own stories and personas—I already have my next book started!

1. Short man syndrome

Unfortunately, in my career I've worked for more of these men than I can count. And it's **not actually** about height, it's about **insecurity**, because some of the men I have most admired in my career have been on the shorter side of American male height charts. At one of my early bad jobs out of college, I was forced to sit in the same small office as the owner of the small business, with our desks face-to-face. I found out over the first weeks that my uncomfortable desk had just been vacated by my predecessor, who had been having an affair with this same (married) man. Was I expected to be next? The reason my most recent predecessor left was that the owner had started having an affair with the also-married woman in the next office! Holy hell! This was way before sexual harassment was taboo; this was back in the early 1980s. When he wasn't at a long lunch with his current conquest, he would walk around the office with his chest puffed out, then sit down and literally stare at me through his crossed fingers, as if his gaze would cause me to succumb to his irresistible upcoming advances. (It didn't work with me, I acted as if I had no idea what was going on until I could get a better job.) Through the years, I worked for many other men with short-man syndrome they each projected a huge ego with Hitler-like propensities. **Remember, this is a persona, and it only applies to some men, no matter what their height.**

2. Tall man syndrome

Tall man syndrome can strike women, too. They throw their height, weight, physical strength, or girth around to wordlessly intimidate others and inflate their own sense of self-importance. They take up too much space in meetings, they're usually late because hey, no one would dare start without **them**. They infringe on other people's personal space by standing or sitting too close, they feel free to rifle through others' offices when they're away, or call their direct reports on their cell phones any time of day or night that they damn well feel like it. They are often office yellers who get set off at the slightest provocation and don't care who's listening. We know these today as toxic narcissists.

3. Glittery dead-eyed snake women

You can tell the moment you meet one of these women that they would strike out and kill your career with absolutely no compassion or compunction at a moment's notice. They internally run on the emotion of jealousy, always comparing themselves to others in their climb to the top, but outwardly they appear reasonable and very professional. They swallow people whole, usually other women, and mercilessly destroy anyone who dares to get in their way or, in their limited perception, "look better" than them even for even **one** split second. They care only about themselves and their own interests. If they are not the business owner, they have the owner completely snowed about how great they are.

4. CEO sociopaths

These men and women at the very top position and rung of the ladder truly think they are better than everyone else. Everyone should bow to their power. They give orders, and they don't listen. God's gifts, overpaid. According a study dating back to 2010, there were at least three times as many psychopaths in executive or CEO roles than in the overall population. But more recent data found it's now a much higher figure as high as 20 percent.

5. Womanizers and other addicts

(See also number 1.) I kid you not, I've worked for more of these than any other negative persona. Some men in positions of leadership seem to need to have affairs with every woman possible. It took a lot of skillful parrying to avoid them in my youth. I've observed (and reported) men that kept entire meetings with multiple important parties waiting for hours in conference rooms while they were out philandering with their latest work conquest. (For those interested, the result of one of my most strident complaints was weeks of useless "organizational development meetings" while HR did nothing whatsoever about this particular offender.) If they're not having sex, they're using drugs or alcohol. I worked for one alcoholic guy that was like the movie "Groundhog Day." Every morning, he would show up, clasp his hands and ask me, "What are we doing today?" Because he literally didn't remember anything at all from the day before. Newsflash, no one should have to do your thinking for you.

6. Scumbag "jokesters"

At an early job, I worked for a guy in his 40s with gray-speckled hair that was permed into an afro, he wore tight polyester leisure suits, and gold-rimmed aviator-style glasses with tinted lenses. He liked to tell hilarious jokes around the office, usually with a punchline about how pussy smelled like fish. (In terms of timeframe, this was during the time Clarence Thomas was harassing Anita Hill.) A lot of this has stopped in companies due to sexual harassment lawsuits and the #MeToo movement which was long overdue. But there are many other toxic men and women still telling jokes around the office that are actually barely-disguised sarcastic criticism of others, aren't polit-ically-correct, or which demotivate, and sometimes appall, everyone around them. Employees feel as if they have to "laugh" or else not fit in to the toxic corporate culture. And my goddess, an entire political party is trying to put an admitted "pussy grabber" back in office right now. How did he ever get there in the first place?

7. Sly self-enrichers

Both men and women fall into this category. I worked for one man who decided to spend 75% of my advertising budget on a pro base-ball team executive suite, not because it would really help business, but because he wanted to be able to take advantage of it with his personal family and friends. I once worked with a woman—VP of sales—whose every decision benefited only her husband whom she had managed to convince us to hire; he also did all of the heavy thinking for her. (Shame on our CEO for allowing it to go on for years until she was finally fired despite dozens of complaints.)

8. Short-term myopics, a.k.a. quarterly-profit quarterbacks

I once worked for a public company that bought market share for a new digital product category just to "look good" for one quarter. For a gain of two points, they were willing to lose $4 million. I doubt Warren Buffett invested in this company. Thank goodness, because they went under right after Halliburton declared bankruptcy for their first time in 2003 during George W. Bush Jr.'s administration. Good times.

9. The rich and talentless

I've worked for some CEOs who buy talent like they collect art. These people **wish** they were talented, so they hire talented people--and then spend all their time criticizing them and tearing apart the work done on their behalf. Funny how none of them ever came up with a single creative idea on their own.

10. Power junkies

Most of the time, people at the top have put in some time to be there. But sometimes, they just marry in, or inherit the business. The power junkie may have some skills, but they mostly just have an entitled atti-tude. They wear the best clothes and drive the best cars and eat at the most expensive restaurants and they want everyone to know how rich and important they are. They helicopter in and make poor decisions based solely on their own egos. Because they can.

11. Do-nothing, care-nothing, absentee bosses

At one of my first sales jobs, I went into my boss's office and asked him in all earnestness about the benefits of our product so that I could better counter sales objections. His answer was, "Tell them anything to sell it." He was there in the office every day, but not really, because he did not care. At a recent job, I worked for a guy who came in one morning a week, sometimes less, yet he insisted that every decision be his. He truly didn't care about his customers or his employees, he just wanted money to keep rolling in. Which it did, due to the dutiful efforts of the hogtied people in his employ and the lack of competition in his industry. Imagine the profits he would have enjoyed if he showed up, gave a shit, and empowered others to make decisions.

12. Hermits and decision-phobic limp rags

These people are natural introverts and have a very hard time making decisions. They spend a lot of time looking for data, they follow what other companies have done rather than try anything innovative. They talk to multiple people soliciting varying opinions about the same topic, then they follow no one's advice. They change their minds a lot, and tend to agree with everyone—that is, to their face. They prefer that other people make decisions because then they can blame someone else if things go wrong. They only achieve minimal success; their companies are usually considered as mediocre as they are.

13. Overly nice guys and gals

These are the people that are difficult to see as problematic at first, because they are so very nice. In reality, these people-pleasers usually have their own agenda going on which is hidden, even from themselves. They're martyrs and doormats, and exhibit passive-aggressive behaviors like "forgetting" lots of things. They would be more helpful to companies if they were more honest and were able to say no, albeit in a productive way. I was married (as well as being a business partner) with two of these sorts, their overly-nice personas often implied that I was the bad guy when they said nothing and let me do the public truth-talking on tough topics we had already agreed upon in private. I was often blamed for things behind my back so that they could save face and continue to be the nicest of all nice nice-guys. (Sometimes good-cop bad-cop is a strategy, sometimes nice guys use it as a default setting even when it's detrimental.) I still get blindsided by these sorts of characters. NOTE: They don't "do it on purpose."

14. Cunning kiss-asses

Everybody knows these people for what they are; they need little explanation. These women or men—generally middle managers or VPs—behave one way to the whole firm, and a completely different way to the big boss. Everyone can see right through them, but the big boss is completely snowed. Often, they worm their way into supposed personal friendships, but only with people that can help them get ahead. For everyone else, they make every day a profound misery with public slap-downs, calling yet another "standing" meeting, or getting furious if anyone else but them dare have a direct conversation with the big boss. (Also see #3 and #7.)

15. Insecure ninnies

These people are deathly afraid of others outperforming them. Sometimes these people are business owners who have no degree, weren't that good in school, or aren't really that smart or talented. Sometimes these people are managers who have no background or experience in the role they've been promoted into. These very insecure people cannot allow anyone else to shine. They surround themselves with underlings, sycophants, and yes-men, and are rarely able to achieve high levels of success as a result.

Harvard Business Review recently offered to solve my "office politics insanity" for only $19.95 via email. **"How to work productively with your colleagues for the good of your organization and your career."**

- Gain influence without losing your integrity
- Contend with backstabbers and bullies
- Work through tough conversations

- Manage tensions when resources are scarce
- Get your share of choice assignments
- Accept that not all conflict is bad
- Arm yourself with the advice you need to succeed on the job, from a source you trust"

The same day, I received another email from a local creative recruiting agency:

"Saboteurs. Finger pointers. Belittlers. Spotlight stealers. Do you work with any of these kinds of people? If so, you're not alone. According to a <u>recent survey</u>, 31 percent of advertising and marketing executives interviewed said a coworker has tried to make them look bad on the job. The good news is that the figure is down from 50 percent in 2008, when TCG conducted a similar poll. Still, the fact that nearly one-third of survey respondents feel the need to watch their backs at work is noteworthy."

Here's the thing, when you get to know most people, you find out that they are not really what they project at work at all. They've probably been beaten down and are leaning on childhood survival patterns in order to survive. Inside we're all made of the same stuff. But meanwhile, we've created a lot of nasty 3D avatars that pose as "leadership."

It is the <u>top leaders</u> of people—C-suite executives, business owners and managers—who need to change the toxic environments in their workplaces, not middle managers or employees. One cannot lead from below. You need to fire when necessary, mandate and verbalize a better corporate culture, and model good behavior at all times. A wry and kind sense of humor can go a long way, too.

If you recognize yourself as a toxic leader with one of these false toxic personas, you **know** you are not happy, you are fearful and insecure, just like everyone else. You are **not** living your dream, even if you have expensive cars, artwork, golf club memberships, and homes in every city. You know inside yourself that you are not being a good person, and you feel guilty underneath it all for the daily work hellhole you have created.

The good news is, you can change. Start now.

On the other hand, if you are a sociopath, you probably know it but don't care. But be warned that you are seen accurately, and your pretense may need a brush up. Try pretending to be a better person with a conscience and morals so that you can be more successful and appear better than you actually are. But you'll have to be consistent not to be discovered. Know that any false move will be very apparent to everyone within your company, and they will all turn secretly against you. (Sweet dreams. No doubt you have a golden parachute so you'll be fine as a social pariah or with money-grubbing posers surrounding you.)

Chapter 5

Are CEOs sociopaths?

There have been a lot of articles published about the number of CEOs who are sociopaths or psychopaths.

An article in _Psychology Today_ defines psychopathy as a spectrum disorder, with the highest on the spectrum exhibiting a lack of conscience or empathy. What's dangerous about the worst ones is that they can often appear quite charming—on the outside.

The article goes on to define the difference between sociopaths and psychopaths: "The terms 'psychopath' and 'sociopath' are often used interchangeably, but a 'sociopath' refers to a person with antisocial tendencies that are ascribed to social or environmental factors, whereas psychopathic traits are thought to be more innate."

Are you a psycho? Unlike other disorders, if you have to ask whether you are a psychopath or not, your chances are 50/50—you may or may not be, because when you operate without a conscience, you literally cannot tell the difference.

"It has been estimated that approximately 1 percent of males and 0.3-0.7 percent of females could be classified as psychopaths." That means there could be more than <u>3 million</u> in the United States alone, and 70 million worldwide.

Tomas Chamorro-Premuzic, a professor of business psychology at University College London and at Columbia University, an associate at Harvard's Entrepreneurial Finance Lab and author of "Why Do So Many Incompetent Men Become Leaders? (And How to Fix It)" said in an article in 2019, "According a study dating back to 2010, there were at least three times as many psychopaths in executive or CEO roles than in the overall population. But more recent data found it's now a much higher figure: <u>20 percent</u>."

So, what's a poor psychopath or sociopath to do? Maybe you can fake it better.

Here are some things you can do as a leader to pretend you're not a psycho. Or as <u>Fortune</u> magazine puts it, "how to rebuild trust" in the aftermath your abject failures, particularly after the economic mess you created in 2008 and the epic incompetence you displayed in 2020.

1. Take a stand and be personally visible in discussing issues like income inequality, sustainability or climate change.

2. Communicate about how much you care about the community and how great you treat your employees because they are important to you. Do this with shareholders, but more importantly, with your employees directly.

3. Pretend that you are human and relatable; that you have personal values and have overcome obstacles to attain your success. Even though most people wrongly think that competence, intelligence and talent are the most important traits in the professional world— they aren't. The most important are warmth and trustworthiness, according to <u>Harvard Business School professor Amy Cuddy</u> and her fellow psychologists Susan Fiske and Peter Glick.

Pretend that you place the customer ahead of profits and that you truly care about them as well as your employees.

Chapter 6

Compensation

In the last few years, there has been a great deal of awareness about wage and wealth disparity in America. According to CNN in 2020, CEOs made 299 times more than their average worker. In 2023, it was 344.4 to 1 according to <u>Statista research</u>.

Robert Reich, former United States Secretary of Labor, shared this on social media:

CEO-to-worker pay ratio:

> Coca-Cola: 1,621-to-1
> Levi Strauss: 661-to-1
> McCormick & Co: 585-to-1
> Carnival: 490-to-1
> Unisys: 313-to-1
> Tyson Foods: 294-to-1

Does anyone else see a problem with this picture?

Dan Price, CEO of Gravity Payments in Seattle, became famous for cutting his own salary and making the minimum starting salary for everyone at his company $70,000. Although he was panned by conservatives and conservative hate media, his company has been enormously successful. He told _Newsweek_ in April of 2021 that he had tripled his revenue since he had raised salaries six years prior.

A famous study at Princeton backed Dan Price up—if you add $5,000 per year to that $70,000. The study's conclusion was that money did indeed buy happiness, but only up to $75,000 per year. Apparently after that, your day-to-day experience doesn't improve that much as your income grows, but your "life satisfaction" does. Bring on the life satisfaction please.

Mr. Price, very active on social media, posted these great questions:

How come CEOs get million-dollar bonuses for reaching their goals while workers get a pizza party?

How come CEOs get more for being fired than workers get for working?

How come CEOs get paid in stock that's not taxed while workers get taxes taken straight out of their paycheck?

How come CEOS get to work from home while sending workers back to the office?

How come CEO pay has grown 1,167% since 1978 while worker pay has grown 14%?

How come CEOs get private jets while workers are lucky to get a subsidized bus pass?

How come when a CEO retires they get a $1 million-a-year pension for life and when a worker retires they get a cake?

Disgracefully, women still earn 78% of what men earn in America for the same work. In 2017, Google was sued by the Department of Labor for discriminating against women in the extreme.

Shameful. And in this day and age of social media, very public.

Take careful note: the boycotting of companies due to their business practices, political "donations" and bigoted beliefs has only just begun. New state regulations to address salary discrimination, including transparency laws passed in New York since the Google case, allow workers to inquire about, discuss and disclose wages to one another and to the public. Several studies show a link between pay transparency and an increase in work performance and job satisfaction.

A couple of words to end this chapter with. 1) Sales goals and 2) Bonuses.

Sales goals are great, as long as you are in the trenches with your sales staff and understand the economic realities of your industry. If you arbitrarily set sales goals and then get angry, demote, or fire people who don't reach your arbitrary sales numbers, then fuck you. Seriously. You don't get it, you've never read a book about sales or marketing, and you should go out of business.

Regarding bonuses. Most companies go along all year sharing no information, then right before Christmas, decide whether or not they will hand out a hundred dollars or give out turkeys. It's a sham and everyone knows it; they know you're just a cheapskate and that's why your turnover is so high. (Your entire staff is looking for another job right now.)

The best company I have ever worked for is completely transparent all year about sales numbers, bonuses all staff based on results each and every month, and encourages all staff by reminding them about how much they contribute to the bottom line. Give it a try. This company is consistently, outstandingly successful for a reason.

Chapter 7

Perks and Benefits

B esides paychecks, other perks and benefits can help attract and retain top employees. In addition to health care benefits and 401(k) plans, holidays, paid time off and "<u>unplugged</u>" vacation time has become more important to employees looking for a work-life balance.

The research says that company cultures that support unplugging have "employees that are more engaged and more likely to report feeling that their employer cares about them as a person (64 percent to 43 percent) and that their job is important (73 percent to 57 percent). Forty percent of employees in cultures that do not support unplugging are looking or planning to look for a new job in the next year."

"<u>Sleep deprivation</u> has become the norm in American businesses, but it is a serious hazard, producing the same effects as alcohol intoxication. American employers and employees still tend to believe the key to getting more done is simply to do more or work harder. This belief is so pervasive that some workers fear to admit or how tired they are, afraid others will see them as weak or unable to cope."

The truth is—backed by science—that overwork, chronic stress, fatigue or constantly working overtime is not a badge of honor or success. In fact, it's quite detrimental, negatively affecting the prefrontal cortex responsible for logic and good decision-making. And you won't necessarily know you're in trouble.

In fact, sometimes overtime is lethal, even for white collar employees. In 2024, a former Green Beret who worked at Bank of America dropped dead because of too much overtime mandated by a boss, despite warnings by the firm's HR department, as reported by the Wall Street Journal. One worker quit after being kept at her desk until 5 a.m. consistently while her boss told her to lie about it.

Nice, huh.

Companies have tried in recent years to think outside the benefits box, some successfully, and some less so. For instance, it's been found recently that "wellness benefits" have not been utilized or appreciated as much as initially thought when they were first offered.

However, four-day workweeks have been a resounding success in every trial.

Studies of workers in other countries—including Australia and Sweden—show that a 22- to 30-hour workweek is "ideal" and can actually create higher productivity and a healthier workforce. Whether it's a 6-hour workday or 4-day workweek, employees get sick less often, have lower stress, and work harder with greater focus.

Even in workaholic Japan, in June of 2021 the <u>Japanese government</u> recommended that companies implement four-day workweeks. The government is hoping that families opt to have more children and spend more money during their extra free time.

In <u>Iceland</u>, the results were overwhelming. Trials of a four-day week in which workers were paid the same amount for fewer hours took place between 2015 and 2019; productivity remained the same or improved in the majority of workplaces.

What have you done in terms of compensation and benefits for your employees? Have you tried unlimited PTO? Sounds like a great perk, doesn't it? Apparently, it's a ruse. It's actually a money-saving policy because it means companies don't have to pay you for unused vacation/PTO/sick days when you leave the organization, and studies show that American workers are afraid to take time off so there's a double win.

Wow. Good job, sociopath! Go back to the drawing board. Read a book or an article. Even if it's not this one.

Chapter 8

Stupid, Useless Meetings and Closed-Door Bullshit

While all of us working stiffs know that meetings can be one of the most productive ways to conduct business and get a group up to speed, we've all had to endure the opposite—i.e., stupid, useless meetings, horrific all-staffs and closed-door bullshit. These are a bane and a time drain, and ridiculous meetings and their organizers are often the butt of company jokes, serious grumblings at the coffee machine, or worse, the start of an employee exodus.

Don't confuse **holding** a meeting with actually **accomplishing something**. Big mistake.

So how do you have a **productive** meeting? Well, first you have to know what you want to accomplish. What is the purpose of your meeting? Spell out the goal or objectives of a meeting as well as listing all agenda items right in the meeting invitation. That way afterwards you can gauge whether or not a meeting was a success, or even necessary in future. Hopefully you'll be reaching decisions that everyone in the meeting needs in order to move ahead.

Keep everyone to the agenda **unless** they're digressing to topics that are truly important to people. Don't be a jerk and cut people off in a false and also egotistical dictatorial way because **you** created the agenda; allow the meeting to feel comfortable and respectful to all parties. Take notes and send out a short summation to all attendees when the meeting is over.

And another thing. Inform the rest of the applicable staff—who weren't invited—about what was discussed, determined and decided at the meeting. Be aware that the rest of the people **not** in your meeting always subliminally feel left out. Make sure they are briefed and feel part of the whole process, and that they feel important too. Such a simple thing to do. Why does pretty much no one do this?

Closed door meetings are especially stressful for the rest of your staff. They are thinking the worst, so be aware and be compassionate about this—allay their fears. Make sure they know topics discussed and outcomes—and double or triple your job satisfaction and productivity.

I'm sorry, but doesn't this seem like common sense and common human courtesy to you? Avoid closed-door meetings as much as possible.

I've worked for companies that claimed to have an "open-door policy," but every single day "leaders" shut their doors all day long, causing a tense and very uncomfortable atmosphere for everyone. I've also worked with people who seem to live for the "power" of holding "important" closed-door meetings with smug, self-important looks as they stride to the next.

Thankfully, I don't work with, or for, them anymore!

To recap:

- Create a written purpose for each meeting

- Create a list of agenda items sent with the meeting invitation

- Create a safe space and encourage all attendees to participate, even normally quiet people

- Stick to the agenda, unless something really important is being discussed—in that case, don't be an asshole and cut people off

- Take notes and send a summation afterwards to all attendees, along with whether or not you felt goals and objectives were achieved

- Brief the rest of the staff and team who weren't at the meeting about what transpired, especially if important decisions were made—and most especially if it was a closed-door meeting

Some "leaders" tend to monopolize conversations at meetings and throw their weight around. They use meetings to criticize employees' or managers' actions either blatantly or backhandedly. In these sorts of meetings, only certain number of people feel brave or safe enough to speak up and contribute or put forth any good ideas they may have—which is yet another team atmosphere and leadership **fail.** While not listening and using meetings as a public stage for your own ego, you are demotivating everyone and losing out on your greatest brain trust—your staff.

If no one ever says anything in your meetings other than praise or nodding "yes," you can be certain you are doing meetings wrong. A good leader asks for other opinions, they don't use meetings to pontificate, berate others or praise themselves.

And remember this—your meeting's purpose should **always be positive**.

Always praise in public, and correct in private. Always treat everyone as an individual, and do not lump your entire staff together. This is Management 101, and it's shameful how few leaders don't know or practice this basic precept.

Chapter 9

Horrid Emails, Or Even Worse, Announcements Via Internet

A quick email sent by a happy person can save oodles of time. An email sent by a toxic "leader" is an epic time-waster, as you sit reeling for minutes having been slapped down by a heinous bitch or bastard, and then you struggle pretty much all day and perhaps a sleepless night or two to regain your self-esteem, especially if there were some significant people copied in the cc line.

Get over yourself, you're the one who actually **sucks,** not the recipients of your nasty, public correspondence.

Another thing for everyone to heed, don't spend time composing email after email until the thread back and forth is 20 or more responses to responses, resulting in an unintelligible and impossible to follow cluster-fuck of "I have no idea what to do now." For god's sake, get the person on the phone, what do you think that constantly updated extension list is for? Or better yet, get off your ass and go see them in person and build a better team atmosphere. Take them a piece of chocolate or something, try being a human being even if it doesn't come naturally to you.

Emails are not communication—communication is a **two-way street**. If your words aren't received accurately, that's on you. Go clear things up.

Besides, as everyone should know (but most don't), roughly 93 percent of communication is non-verbal. Which means that emails pretty much suck to start to start with. According to UCLA professors Mehrabian and Ferris from their article published in the *Journal of Consulting Psychology* in 1967, the relative importance of words used, tone of voice and body language to someone's understanding of a message was 7%, 38% and 55% respectively. Emails are just words—7% important to someone really "getting" and receiving your communication accurately.

Just keep that in mind when you are typing—**before** you hit send.

Do not send a blanket email berating everyone in an entire department or company when it's actually one or two employees which have done something you don't want them to do. Communicate individually. Or maybe rather than admonishing someone, perhaps you could learn better communication skills. Or actually make their job description clearer to them or something like that.

Anyway, what's worse than a bullshit blanket email? Well, it's getting fired online. Braden Wallake posted himself bawling while announcing layoffs on LinkedIn and Vishal Garg held a Zoom meeting firing 900 right before the holidays.

Don't be like Braden or Vishal, FFS.

Chapter 10

Org Charts / Work Flow Process / Clusterfuck-ed-ness

S ince this is a very general book replete with my own experience, naturally you will need to extrapolate it for your particular business model. Manufacturing is one thing, construction is another thing, online product sales is another thing, service businesses are yet another. But we can always learn from other people's mistakes.

Many times, the worst corporate problems are structural or process-related, and company leadership is blind to this part of what they need to observe, fix, constantly adjust to, and manage.

For instance, one company I worked for refused to have the engineering design department review plans until **after** a project was sold, even though the engineering design was critical to the ultimate pricing and the final workability of a project. And **even though** engineering too often found a problem that would kill a sale after the contract was signed, leaving a very unhappy customer and a very disappointed salesperson in the lurch. Major fail in process, and fail to the leader who **never listened**.

The engineering design team should have been made part of the sales team. But that had "never been done;" the design team was "part of operations" so no one was allowed to try it.

In a different scenario, the first company I co-owned, we had a major structural elephant in the room. My partner did all his own creative work on his own accounts which were legacy clients. Sometimes he would "let" someone work on a small aspect of a project he was working on.

I was the one bringing in all the new accounts, all the clients, and all the profitable business that kept us growing. Yet the entire creative staff reported to my lone-wolf partner, not to me. No matter how many project management tools and review process steps I implemented, the fundamental problem was that everyone critical to my projects and work flow **reported to someone else**, and therefore didn't have to meet "my" deadlines or "my" creative parameters based on client expectations.

My salary was based solely on commission during the early years, and I actually lost clients due to obstinate and back-stabbing behavior by salaried people who didn't report to me. ("We can't change our concept!" Even if it is 30% over the client's budget!) My partner worked completely outside the system of the rest of the agency to undermine me daily. But I was too young and dumb to realize the real problem until years later. I allowed my partner to make me into a bad guy, while my partner was the super nice guy. Am I bitter? Yeah, you could say that. You could also say, "divorce number one."

But learn the real lesson here, people, because it's a big one, it's not about me. It applies to a lot of crappy companies out there right now making people miserable on a daily basis. The problem is structural. Fix your fucking org charts.

Too few companies figure out how their work needs to flow, who is the most capable of making good decisions in a timely manner, and where redundancies are that are a hinderance to productivity. Their organizational charts are mostly based on egos (here we go with the toxic personas again), and they never seem to ask the people actually doing the work how to fix things. They don't acknowledge process problems or overlaps. NOTE: Overlapping responsibilities are fine, as long as clear chain of authority and method for resolution of conflict is laid out.

An organizational chart needs to reflect what's really going on.

I worked at one firm where literally nothing moved forward because the owner, who made every decision large or small, might unexpectedly throw a fit of temper and change directions completely on a whim. And often he was then gone without warning for weeks upon weeks at a time, so that no decision whatsoever got made and nothing moved forward. Talk about the most unproductive job and company I ever saw and didn't fit into. I'm a doer and I accomplish a lot. One job I left, when I worked for a major newspaper, replaced me with five different positions. Another VP job I left replaced me with three people plus an outside consultant—not to mention spending a shit-ton of money on outsourced projects that I could actually complete without any help during my tenure there. I told the CEO I saved him big bucks all the time, but he never believed me, and he certainly never compensated me. So, I quit and went to work for a better CEO.

And he paid through the nose. Yeah, still bitter about that one, too, because later he also fucked over a lot of my colleagues who were my friends.

Watch for your key people—the ones that really do the work. Because I'm not the only one. There are millions of excellent but demotivated, underutilized employees longing to work in a great environment but stuck in a shitty job with a shitty boss right now.

That's on you.

Chapter 11

Reasonable and Clear Assignments / Tasks / Job Descriptions

If you're in a leadership role, do you find yourself redoing every assignment given to one of your employees? Do your employees know how their assignments fit into department goals, or overall corporate goals? Do they actually know what they have been hired to do?

Maybe they're working blind because you don't tell them everything they need to know. Perhaps you're even one of those people who dismisses questions because "you're too busy" and "they don't need to know that." How unbelievably stupid and egotistical you are. You're probably so insecure that you relish the fact that "no one can do the job as well as you can."

Get a grip, **you** are the problem. Your job as a leader is to set the goals, set the standards, define the benchmarks for success, get your staff the help they need to do their jobs right the first time with excellence, and then get out of their way while you keep looking out ahead to create the next vision.

Your job is **directly reflected** by your staff's results. And if they aren't performing up to par, get out a big mirror, because most likely it's **you** that needs to alter your course.

Too many people sit wondering what their bosses are thinking, and wondering what their priorities are. What's the most important thing to do right now, this week, or within the next month or quarter?

Some people are very self-directed, particularly people who've been entrepreneurs. I know I have a list of tasks going at all times, which includes things I think the company needs to do even if it's outside of my supposed scope of work.

If you are the current owner or CEO of a growing business, you may have a completely different problem. You can't let go—you know all too well what the issues are. You may be unsure about how to get to the next level. Maybe you're not good about communicating or motivating or bringing in more resources besides just yourself. It can be hard to know what to delegate and who to delegate to.

People who **start** good companies aren't necessarily automatically good at **growing** them, because they're not necessarily good leaders of other people right off the bat. (Some lucky ones are.) But, I have never really seen a case where an entrepreneur can successfully hire managers to grow a company **for** her without her involvement; usually if that's tried there's an eventual falling out.

Therefore, **I think entrepreneurs have to learn new skills along the way**: good leadership strategies and motivating and managing people to do their best. The ones who study and practice good leadership are the people who win and build successful companies for the long-term.

We all want to work for and with "that guy!" And the proverbial Warren Buffetts of the world want to invest in them, too.

It takes work to really think things out and delegate and provide leadership opportunities to your staff. Get off your ass and learn new skills.

Chapter 12

Office Atmosphere / Corporate Culture

―――――――――――――――――

For the average office worker, the comic strip called "Dilbert" by Scott Raymond Adams sums up the atmosphere within a lot of organizations. Most corporate cultures belong in a petri dish. And artificially trying to activate a nonexistent company culture is a joke, and only adds to an already stifling and unsatisfying office environment.

For instance, there are the obligatory office birthday cards grudgingly signed by people you barely know. (How fast can I, as the birthday girl, throw this in the trash without looking bad?) There are the "team building" activities like rock climbing, bowling, or bungee jumping. (No thanks!) And it's not just coffee anymore; there are company provided "breakfast and snacks" in the company breakroom that are supposed to help people work harder and never take actual breaks. And how about those "let's celebrate" emails from HR about people's work anniversary dates that no one responds to.

Don't even get me started on the company-wide implementation of some fake "rah-rah" slogan on banners and posters that never works.

Here's an idea. Instead, why doesn't the leader of the person experiencing a work anniversary take them **out to lunch** and explain why they are so grateful for their years of service? As a "leader," don't you know that people value being VALUED more than anything else?

While you're at it, why don't you ask them some questions to find out what their ideas are for improving the company?

Have you ever considered regular raises, which almost no one gets anymore? How about bonuses for especially effective and proficient employees? You certainly spent a lot of money trying to fill their positions when they leave! Why not try to keep and motivate them? How about some extra time off with pay, or inviting them on a company incentive trip?

I recently learned about a story concerning Trader Joe's, which is one of the few examples I've ever heard about of how to do things right. A long-time VP was leaving the company, and to thank her and show her how valuable her contribution had been to the organization, management was going to take her and her plus-one on an all-expenses-paid trip to Italy to spend a week with some of their best food and wine suppliers. Unfortunately, the trip was canceled because it was 2020 and Italy was the epicenter of the pandemic. So, what happened, you ask? Did they forget about it, and her? No, they did not. They took her and her brother this year, in 2024, four years later.

A great company with a great corporate culture rewards its best and brightest, and keeps its word, even when it doesn't have to.

Chapter 13

About Cubicles

Let's go over a few more things about the shitty brick-and-mortar office atmosphere at most companies.

For instance, are those cubicles really productive? How can anyone really concentrate or deliver their best work with so much loud conversation and commotion going on around them?

But cubicles, ostensibly adopted by most firms to encourage "more conversation and collaboration" don't do that either. Surprise! In late August of 2024 a 60-year-old employee was found dead at her desk. She had been there for four days. Apparently at Wells Fargo in Tempe, Arizona, employees in cubicles never bothered to say "hi" to each other, and even when they "smelled something bad" didn't bother to check in cubicles either. Oh. My. God.

Talk about a sick atmosphere. So sick it was dead.

An Q&A on July 2, 2021 in the <u>New York Times</u> encouraged a job applicant not to ask about whether or not there will be an office, cubicle or open plan because employees "have no say in the matter." Seriously? Well then, that makes "leaders" 100% responsible for their crappy seating arrangements.

For many, the pandemic-required "remote work" (that used to be called "telecommuting") was good riddance to the toxic and unproductive workplace. Yet now, here we are, demanding that everyone "go back" to the way things were before the pandemic

Why?

From a well-researched article in 2016 called "<u>How Open Offices Are Killing Us</u>," it was found that open offices were sicker offices due to the easy spread of germs.

"The more people working in a single room, the more sick days they took. Compared to regular offices, employees working in an open office plan had 62% more days of absence due to illness. And compared to working from home? Well, a survey from Canada Life found those who worked in open plan offices took 70% more sick days than those who worked from home."

In addition to more sick days, the noise factor in an open office is not just an annoying complaint, it actually leads to lower motivation in solving problems. People tend to give up when they are subjected to hours of noise when compared to people working in silence. Employees exposed to office noise were also found to have higher levels of epinephrine in their urine.

"Epinephrine (also known as adrenaline) is involved in the body's "fight or flight" response. Essentially, workers in open offices are under a constant barrage of adrenaline, their bodies telling them to fight or flee. For those who suffer from anxiety disorders, high levels of epinephrine causes increased discomfort, worry, and distress. Over a period of time, the constant high dose of epinephrine leads to a phase of exhaustion where the body starts to experience the more harmful effects of anxiety."

Frequent interruptions and lack of privacy can have the same effect.

An extensive study from Ipsos and Steelcase found that a "whopping 85% of people are dissatisfied with their working environment and can't concentrate."

So, I repeat, why do you insist on an open office environment? Why do you demand people work in the office instead of at home when that's their best choice for their own productivity, and consequently **your company's?**

An interesting article in Forbes by an HR professional in 2017 spilled the beans on the real reason you can't work from home. She said that when she became an HR person in 1984, pretty much everyone predicted that white-collar employees would be working from home and making their own schedules., sitting at Starbucks or on the beach somewhere. That never came true, even with a pandemic, and even though office space is expensive.

She wrote, "The reason you're not allowed to work from home is that fear grips the corporate and institutional landscape, and many leaders are afraid to trust their employees whenever they're out of sight...

You will never get organic teamwork or collaboration out of people who are forced to be in a place they don't want to be."

Is a row of people in cubicles "looking busy" for you the biggest priority at your shitty company?

In July 2021, a company in the U.K. was publicized for their creation of a life-sized mannequin of what the average office worker may look like in 2024. It has a hunched back, red eyes, hairy nose and ears and swollen wrists. Oh, and sallow, eczema-riddled skin related to stress. Is this where we're headed?

And let's not forget all the employees working outdoors, in warehouses or in manufacturing that need better safety and health practices put in place and enforced because their literal lives are in danger every day. Too often, "leaders" cut corners on those, too. I reference Amazon for that, whose lax standards and high number of warehouse deaths sparked an investigation by Senator Bernie Sanders.

Providing a healthy work environment should be a priority for all employers because it's in their own best interests. Duh. Another F for you. For the rest of the people reading this who are not sociopaths, it's the **right thing to do**.

Chapter 14

24-Hour Accessibility

B ecause of text messaging, too many "leaders" feel that their employees should be accessible to their every little thought and whim 24/7—including nights and weekends. Without downtime, people burn out. And no, you are not their highest priority.

Reality check. They are faking their fake-happy required replies to your sudden brainstorm that apparently can't wait. They feel they have to kiss your ass, but they secretly despise you.

In France, there is a law against contacting employees after hours: https://www.good.is/money/france-lets-you-disconnect.

Wouldn't you rather have your staff's actual loyalty and respect? Yes, you say? Then, do your job during working hours so your employees can achieve and maintain some work-life balance. You apparently need balance, too. If you are constantly texting people after hours, most likely you are just insecure and need an ego fix.

If your idea is actually great, it can wait.

Chapter 15

How You Look

I was once interviewed for a job in a tiny, claustrophobic confer- ence room untidily stacked with upside-down file boxes marked in sloppy red magic marker "employee 401k plan files." The impression they made on me was accurate. Their employee reviews online were horrendous and they clearly did not care about employees or their benefits, not to mention personal, private data storage including 401(k) files which most likely contained Social Security numbers.

This was a huge company by the way, with an international presence. The interview was condescending and pointless, and I was the one who frostily thanked them and walked out early.

While it's true that you will be judged by the appearance of your office, this is less important as our lives have become more online and virtual and so many more people are buying goods and holding meetings remotely via Teams or Zoom. Nowadays, you are more likely to be judged by your website, your social media accounts, or the home office bookcases behind your head when you are on camera.

Does that mean you should give up the well-designed and well-ordered commercial brick and mortar facility? That depends on your business model. Do clients want or need to visit you? In that case, how your company looks in person in 3D reality is important. Keep it clean and make it stylish.

But there's another appearance matter you should think about when in person in 3D reality: Dress codes. In today's world in some industries, dressing up can make you appear over-eager and under-qualified. If your CEO is always walking around in golf or workout clothes while demanding everyone else dress up, this is an unspoken tell. Picture the top engineers at Google and you won't envision three-piece suits. Yet some companies still have dress codes in place.

The need for dress codes or rules about outward appearance of clothing cannot be generalized in a book like this. You can only be chided to give it serious thought. In some industries, dressing up is a good thing, like the fashion industry. For others, it's ego-driven nonsense.

Only you as the leader know if having a dress code is actually important to your business or is a stupid relic of the past that you need to ditch.

As an example, let's say you run a repair business. Does your staff go into your customer's homes wearing wrinkled T-shirts and dirty pants with their ass cracks showing? Yeah, not a good thing. Stylish uniforms and a corporate cleaning / laundry service might be the ticket to success for your company. Does your company rely on office visits from important clients? Then yes, a dress code is a good idea.

But let's discuss the most important topic of all when it comes to appearance: Racial, gender, sexual-preference, physical disability or religious discrimination. There's just one word to know here: **NO**. Just no.*

No matter what business you are in, make it a point to become more diverse at every level of your company. This is the way of the future, and you need to get on board now or be left behind.

By the way, why do you continue to pay women much less than men? Why do you overlook them for powerful roles, when often they are the most competent person on your staff? You already know your leadership grade for this, but I like to repeat it: F. It is **you** who are bad at your job. It is you who are to blame. And only you can fix it.

*Special shoutout to Jamie Dimon, CEO of J.P. Morgan who said in September of 2024 that the firm will continue to focus on Black, LGBTQ, Hispanic, disabled and veteran communities. Backlash from certain elements of American society caused the leadership at Molson Coors Beverage Co., Lowe's Cos., Ford Motor Co. and Harley-Davidson to drop their diversity efforts.

"It's good for business; it's morally right; we're quite good at it; we're successful," Dimon said.

Chapter 16

Age Discrimination

One more thing about how you look. Let's talk about age discrimination.

Why? Because I'm old. And experienced. And so are a lot of people — there are 1,000 people turning 65 every single day in America. And right now, lawmakers are talking about raising the Social Security age even higher despite the fact that many people need to continue to work in order to live.

According to Harvard Business Review, companies report staffing shortages at an all-time high of 77%. Meanwhile, people who are 65 or older now represent the fastest-growing segment of the labor force — by far.

You do the math.

Age discrimination is **not being addressed** by most business self-help books or articles, or even legislation for that matter.

Note that age discrimination goes both ways, with young staff members being discounted and older staff being overlooked.

Young employees are the future, and they have been raised using the latest technology. They can be extremely well-read and informed, and have great ideas. But I'm sorry, it is just a fact that the young are inexperienced. You cannot hire an inexperienced person and throw them into an important position with no training and expect great results. It's not fair to your customers, or to them either.

Older employees are experienced and are often deeply knowledgeable about many subjects. Indeed, at top universities and in the highest levels of government, older people are sought out for the most important positions because they are literally the wisest and best. (Unless they have a stutter, in which case, they are publicly humiliated. But I digress.)

Yet for some reason, older, experienced, wiser people are not sought out to help **businesses** succeed. They are actively weeded out of HR hiring searches, and far too many are let go in favor of younger people, even though those younger people tend to be job-hoppers. (Rightfully so, because that's the only way to make more money because our great "leaders" are not giving people raises in order to retain great staff.)

Perhaps that is yet another reason why companies have gone so far downhill in America. There are so many reasons.

As a leader, you can actively encourage older workers to mentor younger ones to the benefit of both as well as to your entire company. Older workers that have longevity at your company can be the glue that has been driving your productivity because of their institutional/

tribal knowledge and brain trust, and you may not be aware of that. Wake up and find out.

However, with all this said, not **all** young workers and not **all** older workers are great at their jobs or have great potential.

It's up to you to assess each individual fairly, regardless of what they look like outwardly. Which is the point of the last two chapters.

Chapter 17

Training and Cross Training

═══════════════════════════

It is amazing to me the number of companies that hire people and throw them into jobs with no training whatsoever. Once, long ago during my college years, my stepdad got me a summer job at a soda bottling factory. I worked a part-time afternoon shift from 2:00 to 8:00 pm.

At 20-years-old with no experience, they put me at the company's main bottling machine, boom, just like that. All I knew was that I had to wear a hard hat. Dozens of 2-liter plastic bottles went around a circular filling machine, culminating in an automatic capping action. They did show me how to lift a heavy bag filled with caps up the ladder to refill the cap feeder, and how to top each bottle off so they visually all had the same level of soda in them coming down the line. But that was it.

My first evening on the job, the 2-liter plastic bottles we were running got all jammed up in my machine—causing the whole line to be down for about two hours. This stopped all work on one side of the entire factory; the other side ran cans.

The service techs who worked on fixing my big bottle-filling machine were the ones who showed me the **OFF** button—it was round and red. (Picture the "easy" button on the TV ads for Staples, it looked just like that.) They told me to hit that button any time a bottle started crunching up, so that the whole machine didn't jam up with crunched bottles and I could fix things before a big problem like this ever even occurred.

How was I supposed to know that—absolutely no one had told me that when I started—one of the most important things to know in order to do my job right and keep the production line running, essential to the productivity of one half of the factory.

Maybe the managers all hated the college girl with the long blonde ponytail working her way through the summer and wanted to get rid of me quickly. I took that as an unspoken challenge. I showed those bastards. After that first day, I became one of their best bottlers, even when we ran glass instead of plastic. So, suck it, Shasta Bottling.

I've had many jobs that were basically the same sorts of no-training situations, where a person not as resourceful as me would have either failed or delivered a lackluster performance.

For instance, here's another example. I started a job where I had three concurrent weeks with an employee whom I was replacing, who was "so busy" **doing** the job before she moved out of state (!) that she "didn't have time" to train me. I had all of six hours of with her.

After she departed, leaving me without any resources in terms of historic work done, approved company verbiage, or where to find anything, the CEO whom I reported to left me sitting by myself for a good two months. I had to try to get a minute with him here or there to ask questions that I didn't really know I needed to ask.

Once again, I trained myself, working my way up into becoming one of the most productive employees at the company. When I left, I gave them three weeks' notice. They didn't even try to hire my replacement so I could train the next person. But I happened to know that they replaced me with a man making twice my salary, and he needed two assistants and several outside firms to do my job. Cha ching, $uckers.

All I had asked for was to be respected and paid fairly. But I wasn't.

How many stories like this can your employees tell about you?

By the way, here's an idea for you, free with this book. One of the most underutilized training opportunities that apparently no one utilizes anymore involves cross training across disciplines. If you have an attitude problem between departments at your company, why don't you consider having the top two troublemakers switch jobs for two weeks? Let them train each other and see for themselves that the other person fulfills an important role, too.

In addition to being a tool you can use to help staff get along and understand each other better, cross training also provides another benefit. With at least one other person on staff who can fill in for them, your employees will be able to take time off with no downtime or disruption to your company's work productivity. They can really relax, and so can you.

No job should be reliant on just one person to fill a role at your company—there should be a backup for everyone. And for the most part, let your staff work out who gets trained to do what. They are the ones who know best how to divvy up the work.

Chapter 18

Micromanagement / Power and Control

Micromanagement is a sure path to failure. Once again, lay out a clear vision, define assignments and roles—explain the **why** and do everything you need to do to support your staff then stand back while they supply the **how** to get their jobs done.

Give them reasonable expectations for success, don't delineate all their tasks. They can figure that part out. Give them reasonable time-lines, too.

Businesses today suck the life right out of employees with their end-less rules and timeclocks. I know people who have been docked for being 10 minutes late, glared at, or publicly called out, even if they were a huge contributor who worked through lunch every single day, or stayed late whenever necessary to complete anything needed.

Shame on you.

One of my friends relayed to me that at her previous job, not only were employees required to have their (monitored) computers on by or before their start time, but they had to pass through (monitored) security beforehand which took an excruciating amount of time, not to mention a long walk through the designated parking lot to get there. **Up to 30 minutes!**

It's a completely stupid emphasis. Productivity should be the only measure of a person's job capability and performance. But most companies don't have those measures in place. They're just sucking up their people's time, and they're wasting their money and going the wrong direction.

I can't tell you how many job interviews I've been on where I ask the question, "For this role, if the person did an outstanding job that exceeded expectations, what would the measures be for that level of success?" My question has **never once** been answered because they have never even thought of that.

By the way, regarding that particular company example above, the one that requires people to be at their computer by a certain time and monitored and docked people who weren't? That company—a private university—got into big financial and legal trouble, and their clients (students) sued them. Big surprise.

Moral: Don't be a shitty company running a scam and treating your employees like shit lest you get dragged down to the level you deserve in the media and the courtroom.

Another hardworking blue-collar man I met got into a serious car accident on the way to work for which he was hospitalized. He was docked pay because he neglected to call in sick **24 hours in**

advance. This is a true story—he worked for a newspaper that I used to work for. Ridiculous doesn't even cover this HR rule; he was apparently supposed to know in advance that he would be in the hospital because he would get in a wreck on his way to work? Stupid. Stupid, stupid. The HR department would not back down, and he was never paid.

The pandemic showed us that many people are in roles where they can work from home, often more productively than they did before, and yet at this point in the post-pandemic world, power-hungry micromanagers are demanding their loyal employees resume their former commutes and be there in their offices without additional compensation or any help with the transition or fallout from COVID. Is this so they can abuse them personally? Is this to prove that "they are the boss?" Is this so they can feel important with a bunch of occupied chairs on display to prop up their fragile egos?

Research in 2023 by the Center for Retirement Research at Boston College found that managers would pay 62 percent more, on average, to **set an inflexible schedule**. Are you kidding me now?

As Dan Price, CEO of Gravity Payments in Seattle puts it, "I don't think we've fully reckoned with how much time companies steal from workers by forcing them to commute for jobs that really don't require a commute. If your company is forcing you back into the office for a job that can be done the same remotely, they are saying they don't care about you and want an extra 1-2 hours unpaid each day.

"Here's a little math behind that: Let's say you work a typical 8-hour day and make $20 an hour. That's $160 a day. But if you're commuting an hour roundtrip each day, you're really spending 9 hours devoted to work. Now your paycheck really works out to $17.78 an hour."

Believe me, your employees see this clearly. And they see right through you. They've either quiet-quit already or they are looking for another job right now.

Chapter 19

Too Many Really Lousy Chiefs Who Don't Listen

===============

NOTE: This is the most important chapter in this entire book. Have you worked for "that" company which has way too many people in middle management who do nothing but go to long lunches and meet amongst themselves behind closed doors, and way too **few** people actually doing any work?

I firmly believe that a good leader won't ask people to do anything they are personally unwilling or unable to do; they're not too good to wash dishes when required.

But here's the biggest hallmark of crappy leaders and shitty middle managers: they don't listen to customers or ask them any questions.

Every CEO, and every marketing and sales manager should spend at least one day per month answering the

phone and meeting directly with customers and experiencing what their employees hear and deal with.

You read that right.

How else will they know what's really going on in order to make good management decisions? Yeah, they don't.

This is the shortest chapter in this book, and I promise you, it is the most important. Spend a lot of time listening to what your customers and consumers have to say. Basic common sense. Which is completely lacking at most companies.

Chapter 20

The Customer and Employee Experience

Every single customer's experience is important. And so is each employee's.

Collectively, the "customer and employee experience" delivered by any company can **all** be laid directly at the feet of the CEO, because they set the stage for it.

Which brings me to another point just mentioned in the most important chapter, why aren't more CEOs and leaders talking to customers on the phone or meeting with them out in the field or seeking out and listening to their concerns?

When you talk directly with customers, you just might learn what your problems with customer experience really are so that you can fix them. You also might learn what your competitors are doing better than you. Or you might get the idea for a company innovation that could be completely disruptive to your whole industry.

In other words, talking to your customers on the frontlines can lead you directly to your next success. Why aren't you doing it?

Every leader worth her salt should be making this a priority and emphasis.

And repeat after me, who decided that computers should answer phones? What a stupid idea. Computers should never answer phones. You should—as often as possible. Or a real person should.

At one of the best companies I've worked for, the CEO impressed me more than he will ever even know. (Yeah, he's pretty much one of the few that I admire.) This CEO mandated that the entire company shut down during business hours to attend a presentation about delivering an excellent customer experience—the type of service they give at the world's top hotels.

I will never forget what I think of as the "pickle training," which covered the treatment of clients as well as coworkers. The mandatory presentation in part explained the approach of a guy named Bob Farrell, who passed away in 2015. Bob cut to the customer service heart of things, creating and repeatedly proving his high-touch, caring approach that he started at his own ice cream parlor and restaurant.

To paraphrase his "Pickle Principle," when you go the extra mile to do what is right for another person, treating them like a person instead of "just another customer," you tap into their emotions—and that's how you deliver the extraordinary, memorable service that builds loyalty. If they ask for a pickle with their ice cream, then <u>give them the damn</u>

<u>pickle</u>. In fact, if you don't have any pickles, jump in your car, run to the grocery store, buy a jar, and come back and add pickles to their ice cream on the spot.

Bend over backwards and touch someone's heart and you have a loyal customer, employee, or colleague for life. Because yes, it's personal. Business is personal.

Chapter 21

Reviews

—————————————

While delivering an outstanding customer experience seems like common sense, it seems to elude a large majority of American business owners and "leaders." Although some of them are starting to realize the power of **online reviews**.

Here's the thing. You might not like online reviews. But they are here to stay. And people continue to pay attention to them. Review sites are the great new equalizers and ways for consumers to deliver the truth about crappy service, shitty products, and terrible leadership.

Consumers can review your company on Google Local, Yelp, Angie's List or on the Better Business Bureau's website. If a company doesn't appear or have a listing on one of these platforms, consumers can usually add one for them anyway. There are dozens more, but these sites have the highest name recognition and largest number of views as of this writing.

Most e-commerce sites also now offer consumer product reviews right on their websites, including Amazon, Target, Home Depot, Wayfair, and many others. And companies like Uber allow reviews to go two ways—a rider can review their driver and the driver can review their rider, too.

Reviews reveal the fact that power is going back to the consumer, and the worker as well, because people searching for jobs can **also** write and read reviews about working conditions. Online sites are offering a great way to strike back at miserable jobs. Employees and former employees can review your shitty company on Glassdoor or Indeed, and other job sites.

And drumroll—some of these sites actually allow ratings for the CEO himself/herself. That's right, your employees and former employees can now tell the truth about **you personally**. Because employee reviews are anonymous, you can still be reviewed regardless of severance agreements you've tried to put in place to cover your many leadership failures. Only if someone actually lies about you or your company can their review be taken down via a legal order.

So, here's a thought. Rather than try to squelch bad reviews and cover up your shitty reputation, why don't you just stop being a shitty leader?

Times they are a changin'. There is another similar phenomenon happening in America. Up until the last few years, unions had been largely destroyed by the richest 1% big business monopolies pushing "right to work" legislation in every state. Now unions are coming back stronger than ever.

To put it another way, your shitty policies will get noticed and workers may decide to do something about it. Remember the Frito-Lay—owned by PepsiCo—worker strike in 2021 against 84-hour workweeks in 90+ degree factory temperatures?

Also, thankfully, the overreach of companies mandating that employees sign noncompete agreements (which meant that people couldn't work for a competitor for a certain amount of time, severely limiting their rights), has been struck down and dismantled. The Federal Trade Commission delivered the final blow to non-competes in 2024.

By the way, if you thought this chapter was about employee reviews, here's a word about those.

Once a year is not enough. You should be praising and giving feedback weekly at the very least. And for goddess' sake, don't ask people to fill put their own damn reviews. What a stupid idea.

You don't need to do a long-form review unless you plan to fire someone. Remember, that's what everyone thinks and fears when it's review season. Reviews are not the way to motivate someone. Spending time and really communicating with employees is what makes them do their best and feel like they have the best job in the world.

Why don't you already know that? Never mind. Just do better. Put yourself in the other person's shoes and figure out what they want. **If they're good and you don't want to lose them, give them a raise.**

Chapter 22

Your Brand

People want to work with and for the best companies. They want to know the details about why they should wear your company's logo. How do you get to be the kind of company that has a brand so well-known and respected that people want to wear merchandise displaying it?

As discussed in the last chapter, **you**, as the leader and embodiment of your brand must be visible and likeable. You must be able to verbalize your value proposition. You do interviews on the news, you are out there, people see you on social media and on videos. There is a distinct personality that is real, that is approachable. It is a personality that people want to be with.

Many small companies have never even send a press release out. They have some young person doing social media, or their son or daughter. Or they micromanage and overthink everything so that nothing gets done.

Many medium and large companies are mired in mediocrity. Often these are the companies who yammer on loudest in meetings about "out of the box thinking" or "raising the bar."

Your brand messaging has to be good, not trite. It has to be truthful. It has to cut through the cacophony of forgettable messages out there.

Here's an assignment for you: Look up what the finest branding and advertising minds of all time said and did. Writer and advertising genius, David Ogilvy. Incredible designer, Saul Bass.

Don't copy your insipid competitors. Do and say something completely unique and creative.

The reason that ad agency TBWA\Chiat\Day was able to create the branding campaign "Think different" for Apple was that Apple truly was different—Steve Jobs demanded it. The story goes that he was recently back with the firm and rejected an ad campaign presented by their then-agency with the slogan "We're back." Jobs said the idea was stupid because Apple wasn't back yet. He sought new campaign ideas from new agencies, which led to "Think different," one of the greatest branding campaigns of all time—a campaign that actually did help bring Apple back.

Never forget that, like Steve Jobs, you are the brand.

And remember: Your ad agency can't put lipstick on a pig. The "Think different" campaign never would have worked for a product that was just a lame copy of a competitor's.

Let me repeat. Brand messaging has to be good, not trite. It has to be truthful. It has to cut through the clutter.

It cannot do that if your company and products are mediocre at best.

Here's an interesting article from 2016, "Brand Admiration Is Earned, Not Given: Here's How to Make It Last Forever" outlining some of the reasons why Sears and Blockbuster failed. Neither one **evolved** or changed to take advantage of market trends or current technology: ie. Amazon online sales versus brick and mortar; Netflix streaming versus DVD/VHS. Take heed.

Finally, while most companies sort-of understand the importance of having a website, they rarely keep their site up to date. Even though every single person does their research online and expects to find current information there. Even though you yourself might expect to find every bit of truthful and current information you need or that ever existed on the internet, you allow your own information about your own company to either be nonexistent or out of date.

FFS. Go read your website right now and make sure it reflects you accurately. Keep it updated. Make sure it reflects your fantastic brand, and superior customer and employee experience. (Did that sound sarcastic? It was meant to.)

Chapter 23

Vision Versus Mission Statements

As a professional writer, I despise "mission statements." Through the decades in my marketing and communications career, I have been assigned to write them too many times to count.

Usually subsequently edited by multiple uncreative executives at the company (who are all competing to impress the CEO), the company mission statement often ends up as a long, windy, utterly boring description of what the company **does** instead of what the company stands for.

"We make wonderful widgets for worthy widget twiddlers in the world-class widget-making industry." Oh boy, that's a mission to live for, isn't it?

As opposed to a mission statement assigned to a staff writer to be watered down later, perhaps the company CEO should consider creating the vision herself and imparting it at every turn, both verbally and by her behavior and actions at all times.

Your company's vision should be a lot like a **story**, which, good news, some companies and brands have recently started to understand

and embrace. Your vision, like a story, should be personal and impart emotion. It should leave everyone who hears it feeling the truth of understanding you and your company's purpose.

In order to get you started, your vision could explain **why** your company was formed and why you do what you do every day, why you are different and/or perhaps why someone should pay money for that.

Your vision doesn't need to be printed on a plaque on a wall somewhere. Maybe it's on your website, but maybe it's not.

As the CEO or president or manager, think of yourself as the avatar for your company. Your vision should be visual. Your vision should be modeled and communicated verbally. As the leader, you should find new ways to express your vision every day until your entire organization lives and breathes it.

Word to the wise: If your company vision includes the words "disruption, creativity and the free expression of ideas," don't close your office door every five minutes while you yell into the phone at someone or scold an employee who had the courage to speak up in a meeting. It's not just bad optics, it's bad leadership. And, obvious to all but you, it's the exact opposite of what your vision is purported to be.

Just like parents raising children, children will do what their parents **do**, not what they say. Employees will follow your example, not your empty words. And your customers will definitely get the message and go elsewhere.

Are you experiencing high attrition of employees and customers? There is a reason for that: **You**. Time to get an inspirational vision and actually live and demonstrate it.

Chapter 24

Outsourcing Fail

—————————————

By now we've all experienced first-hand the horrors of outsourced customer "service." After cursing our way through a computerized "routing" system, which feels a lot like hacking through a rainforest armed only with a pocketknife, we finally speak with someone from another country, whose heavily-accented English is a second language at best. This person has no power to actually resolve any important issue, and often we are livid by the point that we do speak with them. Hey, we've all been there. Most people give up, or just blast companies on social media, review sites, and to their friends.

How did we get here?

According to an abstract written in 2004 by Michael F. Corbett for the *Economist* called, "The Outsourcing Revolution:" "*The first myth about outsourcing is that it's new. Actually, the term dates to the 1970s, when manufacturing companies seeking efficiency began hiring outside firms to manage less-than-essential processes. Today many manufacturers outsource 70% to 80% of the content of their finished products."*

Fast forward to today and we have to ask ourselves the question, does outsourcing really work?

Remember back to the COVID-19 pandemic, when we experienced terrible breaks in the "supply chain" coming from other countries like China, South Korea and Mexico. People who ordered appliances, like refrigerators, washers, dryers, had to wait for weeks or even months for them to be delivered. And that's just one small example. Tariffs also caused chaos in every direction—imports and exports.

More importantly, due to inflation, today in 2024 many people in America can't afford to buy more than necessities, even though we are a consumer-driven economy. This inflation is not caused by supply problems, higher salaries, or an increased cost of goods. Why? Because we can see the enormous profits companies are raking in, going directly into the pockets of CEOs, boards of directors, and stockholders.

In 2004, Corbett said, *"For every 1,000 jobs British Airways sends to India, the airline saves $23 million; and, "A Java programmer earns $60,000 a year in the U.S., but $5,000 a year in India."*

Remember back to your economics class, folks. It was Henry Ford in the early 1900s who first recognized the power of the American workforce to become the driving engine (so to speak) of a consumer economy. It was Ford who first understood that paying workers a livable wage allowed them to be able to spend their money—on his automobiles.

Even though we found out later that he was a horrid, raging anti-Semite, these original ideas still paid off and made him one of the wealthiest leaders in history. He certainly wouldn't have sent jobs overseas; he paid people enough to buy his products right here. Five dollars a day was a lot back then.

Are our nation's current corporate "leaders" actually leading us into sustainable territory? No. Today, sociopathic, golden-parachuted CEOs and their entitled, mostly old-white-male boards of directors are part of America's "elite" 1% billionaires **completely out of touch** with average citizens.

The minimum wage in America is still $7.25 an hour, as it has been since July 24, 2009. Full-time minimum wage workers <u>cannot afford</u> a two-bedroom rental anywhere in the U.S. and cannot afford a one-bedroom rental in 95% of U.S. counties, according to the National Low-Income Housing Coalition's annual "Out of Reach" report.

Not taken into account by America's corporate "leaders," the masterminds of outsourcing: Americans buy most goods and services, and as they lose their buying power, American companies also suffer.

Luckily, governmental leadership and investment in our own infrastructure has brought renewed prosperity to America's middle class. Let's hope Project 2025 Heritage Foundation billionaires—the world's dark money leaders—don't crash our economy again like they did in 2008, as George W. Bush Jr. wrapped up his eight full years in office by engineering the biggest global recession since the Great Depression.

Finally, the worst outsourcing fail may be trying to outsource **thinking** to technology.

Chapter 25

Technology and Automation / AI / Big Data

As the cherry on top of the icing on top of the leadership cake today, the world's worst leaders are now busy trying to replace people with artificial intelligence. In July of 2024, after seeming wholesale adoption and acceptance of AI by everyone in America, the <u>Wall Street Journal</u> pointed out how unprofitable this attempt has been thus far. (Dot com crash redux, anyone?)

I find it deeply disturbing how fast AI was unleashed and then "marketed" to all of us, accepted fatalistically as "inevitable," and then constantly foisted upon us by software like Microsoft, and on browsers like, well, all of them. Even social media pushes us to "let AI write" our comments for us. "Helpful" "note-takers" attend meetings and then regurgitate whatever it is we are each apparently supposed to do next.

I hold the deeply unpopular viewpoint that AI should absolutely not do our thinking for us. Ever.

I believe that AI will never replace the incredible creativity, resource-fulness, and potential for greatness held in the tip of the pinky finger in your average unhoused person shuffling along a sidewalk—a person imbued with the untapped and unnurtured capability to save us all if given half a chance.

AI will never be capable of actual reason or morals, in fact, it's already been found to be masterful at <u>deception and lies</u>, according to scientists, who are unable to explain the phenomenon. Furthermore, its ability to write has been found wanting, to say the least. I've had to rewrite absolutely everything generated by ChatGPT, which I myself have never used and never will. Because guess what, AI is unable to grasp or produce nuance, or make big leaps or connections. It cannot reason, it just regurgitates. (I've gotten at least two job offers on LinkedIn to "train AI" to write for $25 per hour. I'm not the only one; it apparently sends out job offers ubiquitously to those with LinkedIn accounts. No thanks.)

For the real creative stuff—the stuff movies and novels or fascinating concepts are made of—AI will never be as good as people, because it can't feel. It's not alive. It can't breathe, it can't see, it can't hear, it can't taste...it's glorified software no matter what you say. It does not have a soul.

The hubris that people think that an algorithm can even begin to approximate a human being. Please.

Here's another big downside: The server power required by AI sucks up precious resources in a world already stressed by climate change. Climate change may make all of us, including AI, extinct. So, there's that.

And what about technology like self-checkout? Some people love it, and some people hate it. And some companies have already invested in it, then invested **even more** in its removal due to high theft. Oops.

Furthermore, when it comes to technology and AI, it's creepy to be followed around, listened to, and watched 24/7 by advertising and programming. It's enough to make you unplug and go hug a tree, and definitely do the opposite of whatever it is that "big data" thinks you are going to do. Big data is busy analyzing what you have purchased, said on your cell phone, watched, listened to, and/or searched for at every moment because it can process all of that and make algorithmic assumptions about your behavior. Super fucking creepy.

But there's more you should consider. Big data stores consumer names, addresses, emails, cell phone numbers, identification account numbers, Social Security numbers, social media pages, ages, income levels, education levels, parental status, home ownership status, IP addresses, preferences and purchase information collected by websites, third-party automation platforms for websites, social media sites, CRMs, digital advertising clicks, and sales transaction data provided by credit card companies.

The negative side of this big data collection led to the massive legislation passed in the European Union known as GDPR (General Data Protection Regulation) which limits the collection of data and allows consumers to opt out. The fines are enormous; the law went into effect in 2018. The GDPR allows the EU's Data Protection Authorities to issue fines of up to €20 million ($24.1 million) or 4% of annual global turnover (whichever is higher). In 2020, penalties under the GDPR totaled €158.5 million ($191.5 million).

Here in the U.S. in 2019, because of their illegal collection and sale of private information, Facebook was fined an unprecedented $5 billion by the Federal Trade Commission in a settlement that also forced them to update and adopt new privacy and security measures. Big data backlash comes into play both in how your company uses personal data in marketing, and what information you collect and store on your servers, computers, websites, third-party providers and "the cloud" which may be vulnerable to theft or hacking. High level executives need to be put in charge of data security at companies instead of the overworked IT guy in the closet in back. We've all seen appalling articles in the last few years about data stolen from major firms and hackers demanding payments. Even our Social Security numbers were recently hacked!

On the bright side, however, algorithms and software can potentially help us make medical breakthroughs faster. AI can outperform humans in the detection of potential problems on CT scans, MRIs, X-rays, and other medical tests—even photos of skin where it can better detect potentially cancerous skin lesions. But this doesn't mean AI can replace physicians—it can just help them—if its conclusions can be trusted. Because AI should always be overseen by a trained person. Due to its being a lifeless piece of software, it's likely to always make mistakes, because programmers can't think of everything, and programmers themselves program in their own biases.

Is AI dangerous? Yes. It's been unleashed without oversight. The very people who developed it have all warned us. Supervision by humans is critical.

But CEOs press ahead anyway, greedily picturing all that "extra overhead" they can cut, savings that can line their own pockets or provide stock buybacks. Some "leaders" listen to no one, have no wisdom, and are unable to think past the next quarter. A particularly offensive and heinous editorial from 2021, published in Dallas News threatened workers that if they didn't get back to work in the office regardless of COVID-19, they might not get a job at all because they would be <u>replaced by robots</u>. What a beautiful red-state attitude.

The thing is, the same workers that CEOs want to replace with machines—the people providing valuable labor—are also the engine that drives our economy. You know, the people who buy things. As in **consumers,** you know. **Your customers.** Here's a brief discussion about that conundrum if you're interested: <u>https://crr.bc.edu/imagining-the-end-of-the-age-of-labor/</u> The fact is that people **buy what they want to buy** with their discretionary funds. Which might not be your steeply, suddenly very overpriced product, like <u>McDonald's recently found out</u>.

And here's another issue that might actually give a selfish leader pause: Your customers do not want AI. This is highlighted by a Discover credit card TV ad running in August of 2024 starring Jennifer Coolidge. In the ad, the company tries to convince Jennifer—their customer—that Discover has **U.S.-based customer service** and that **she's not talking to a robot**.

CEOs take heed. Customers don't like outsourcing, they don't like outsourced customer service, and they don't like talking to AI.

Click your ruby red heels together three times, Dorothy. You see, the answer to your company's potential growth and success has been right there all along. It's the human beings around you—your employees and customers.

If there is one takeaway I hope you really get through your head, it's this. The best leaders pay their people. They listen to their people and their customers. They ask questions, listen, and take action based on what they've learned. I sincerely hope that you are one of them.

The litmus test question for every bit of technology you embrace and pursue at your company should be: **will it help my employees and/or my customers?**

In factories, robotic automation has proven to increase productivity by taking over boring, dangerous, difficult and mundane tasks and allowing manufacturing lines to run 24/7 with no breaks—other than machinery breakdowns, which still require human repair. The machinery still has to be watched over by skilled, knowledgeable people, but it saves their bodies from daily physical pain.

Conversely, when it comes to complex tasks, we have seen only semi-success with artificial intelligence and automation so far. For instance, with self-driving cars: great when the AI works, <u>deadly</u> when it doesn't. Or facial recognition by law enforcement, which has led to wrongful identification and action considered by <u>Congress</u> to limit it.

A company's greatest resource is its people. And that will simply never change.

The underutilization and disrespect of the incredible resource, productivity, desire and intelligence of human beings is our current collective leaderships' biggest mistake. I do not believe this resource will ever be replicated by any machine, no matter how well-programmed.

Why choose **artificial intelligence** when you already have the real thing?

Chapter 26

Working Backward From the End

As a leader or boss, you spend the majority of your time at work, so what are you spending your time on? Are you busy throwing your weight around in a fruitless effort to "prove" yourself to the world, your family, or the father who never thought you'd make it?

Not to be morbid, but we all have the same ending. Eventually we die. What will your obituary say?

More importantly, what is your quality of life right now?

If you are having a hard time "finding people who want to work," you need to know that Gen Z understands that there is more to life than just the drudgery of slave wages to make payments on a student loan they'll never pay off, or save up to purchase a home they can't afford, or spend 12 hours a day at a thankless job they hate.

These people are the next generation—they are **the new leaders in our world**.

So, again, what are **you** doing? How are you spending your time? Is your every waking moment spent struggling to make a name for yourself before your crappy company flames out because your employees hate you and your customers eventually drop you like a rock?

I like to think of working backward when deciding how to spend my time. As in, what are the regrets people talk about when they are on the edge of death? You know, the final point of true wisdom. The international bestseller by Bronnie Ware, a hospice nurse from Australia can give us all some insight. I will paraphrase the top five regrets from her book, The Top Five Regrets of the Dying, in order to help you make better decisions, or you can buy the book yourself.

1. I didn't live my life being true to myself instead of doing what other people expected me to do.

2. I deeply regret spending so much of my life on the thankless treadmill of "working hard."

3. I wish I had had the courage to speak up and express my true feelings.

4. I wish I hadn't lost touch with my friends.

5. I wish that I had let myself feel happier.

About the Author

J.P. Abbott

J.P. Abbott began working at the age of 14, and has spent time at companies both large and small. After graduating from the University of Kansas with a bachelor's degree journalism with a concentration in advertising (or, a B.S. in B.S. as she likes to say) she continued to learn by reading hundreds of books and articles about business, marketing, and leadership. In addition to working at various jobs in corporate America, she also co-owned and ran two small businesses; one of them a luxury home general contractor where she handled the marketing, accounting, interior design and client relations, and one an advertising agency where she advised and consulted with leaders and CEOs in dozens of industries. Improvement is always her goal for herself and everyone around her.